Complicite Associates

A PACIFIST'S GUIDE TO THE WAR ON CANCER

Book by Bryony Kimmings and Brian Lobel

Music by Tom Parkinson

Lyrics by Bryony Kimmings

A Pacifist's Guide to the War on Cancer is a Complicite Associates and National Theatre co-production in association with Manchester HOME. It was first performed at Manchester HOME on 20 September 2016, before touring to Exeter Northcott and the National Theatre London. The original company was as follows:

Director	Bryony Kimmings
Set Design	Lucy Osborne
Costume Design	Christina Cunningham
Choreography	Lizzi Gee
Lighting Design	Paul Anderson
Sound Design	Lewis Gibson
Assistant Director	Debbie Hannan
Creative Associate	Kirsty Housley

Gia	Naana Agyei-Ampadu
Stephen's Mum/Ensemble	Amy Booth-Steel
Dr Lacey/Ensemble	Jenny Fitzpatrick
Mark	Hal Fowler
Emma	Amanda Hadingue
Nurse/Ensemble	Francesca Mills
Laura	Golda Rosheuvel
Nurse/Ensemble	Max Runham
Shannon	Rose Shalloo
Derek/Ensemble	Gareth Snook
Dr Jones/Ensemble	Lottie Vallis
Stephen	Gary Wood

With the voices of Lara Hazel, Gia Jones, Bryony Kimmings, Billy Riley, Victoria Riley, Lara Veitch

Musical Director/Piano	Marc Tritschler
Bass	Oroh Angiama
Guitar	Jon Gingell
Drums	Phil Gould
Violin	Elizabeth Westcott

Production Manager	Niall Black
Company Stage Manager	Heidi Lennard
Deputy Stage Manager	Ian Andlaw
Assistant Stage Manager	Adam Chesnutt
Sound Associate	Tomás O'Connor
Costume Supervisor	Peter Todd
Production Electrician	Laurence Russell
Production Relighter	Tom Mulliner
Sound Operators	Mary Stone, Claire Stamp
Stage Supervisor	David Hill

For Complicite

Producer	Judith Dimant
Associate Producer	Poppy Keeling
Finance Manager	Louise Wiggins
Assistant Producer	Naomi Webb
Communications & Development Manager	Holly Foulds
Project Co-ordinator	Dina Mousawi
Administrative Co-ordinator	Claire Gilbert

For the National Theatre

Dramaturg	Nina Steiger
Company Voice Work	Cathleen McCarron
Deputy Production Manager	Emily Seekings
Wigs, Hair & Makeup Supervisor	Gillian Blair
Wardrobe Supervisor	Jo Kuhn
Lighting Supervisor	Paul Knott
Production Sound	Sarah Weltman
Stage Supervisors	Lee Harrington and Jody Robinson
Rigging Supervisor	Phil Horsburgh
Producer	Ros Brooke-Taylor

Bryony Kimmings is a performance artist, writer and comedian. Previous works have seen her looking at silence around male depression (*Fake it 'til you Make it*), becoming a pop star invented by a nine year old (*Credible Likeable Superstar Role Model*), spending seven days in a constant state of intoxication (*7 Day Drunk*) and retracing an STI to its source (*Sex Idiot*). Bryony has performed all over the world including the Southbank Centre, Melbourne International Comedy Festival, Helsinki Opera House, Croatia, Culturgest – Portugal, Fusebox Festival – Texas and can sometimes be caught doing funnies on telly.

Brian Lobel is a performer, a Senior Lecturer in Theatre at University of Chichester, a Wellcome Trust Public Engagement Fellow and co-director of The Sick of the Fringe. Brian's solo work on cancer (including *BALL & Other Funny Stories About Cancer* and *Fun with Cancer Patients*) has played to tens of thousands of medical students, doctors, patient groups and general audiences throughout the world over the last decade. Outside the world of cancer, Brian performs on a variety of themes and contexts internationally, with venues including Sydney Opera House, Lagos Theatre Festival and Harvard Medical School.

Tom Parkinson is a composer and sound designer working primarily in an interdisciplinary context. He has made the music for over 50 staged works in 20 countries. In addition to Bryony, regular collaborators include the choreographers Keren Levi and Ivgi&Greben and theatre-maker Sharon Smith. Tom has worked with the National Dance Company of Korea, Prague Chamber Ballet, Holland Festival, the National Theatre of Tunisia, the Royal Opera House, the Young Vic, Forest Fringe, Julidans, Phoenix Dance Theatre and Dance Theatre Yekaterinburg. He occasionally writes about contemporary music for *The Guardian* and is currently doing a PhD in music composition at Royal Holloway, University of London.

Complicite Associates is part of internationally acclaimed theatre company Complicite. Through the Associates programme, the Company commissions and produces new work from brilliant theatre makers and artists. Bryony Kimmings is the inaugural Complicite Associate.

Since it was founded in 1983, Complicite has played worldwide, winning over fifty major awards. Recent productions include *The Encounter*, *Lionboy* and *The Master and Margarita*. In addition, the Company runs an award-winning Creative Learning programme.

Artistic Director Simon McBurney / **Producer** Judith Dimant
Trustees Sarah Coop, Roger Graef (Chair), Frances Hughes, Tom Morris, Chetna Pandya, Nitin Sawhney, Stephen Taylor, Sue Woodford-Hollick

The National Theatre is dedicated to making the very best theatre and sharing it with as many people as possible. The National's work is seen on tour throughout the UK and internationally, and in collaborations and co-productions with regional theatres such as Bristol Old Vic, Chichester Festival Theatre, National Theatre of Scotland and Live Theatre. The National's Learning programme offers talks, events and workshops for people of all ages and reaches nationwide through programmes such as Connections and National Theatre: On Demand In Schools.

Chair of the Board Sir Damon Buffini / **Deputy Chair** Kate Mosse
Director of the NT Rufus Norris / **Executive Director** Lisa Burger

Supported using public funding by
ARTS COUNCIL ENGLAND

John Ellerman Foundation

Bryony Kimmings
Writer / Director

Alright dudes. I am a performance artist by trade. I haven't ever made anything with more than two people in it. Those people are often real, not actors (not that actors aren't real). When Complicite approached me and asked if I would like to try and make something bigger, Judith (the producer) was amidst cancer treatment. I said we should make a show about that, and that it should be a musical. I am not a huge fan of most musicals. But I am a very firm believer in form being derived from content and subject matter as opposed to ego or tradition or even really skill set. Cancer had to be a musical. Not in that *Jerry Springer the Opera* way, which was awesome, but now they've done it. Less ironically and more to utilise the medium that has the greatest power to unite huge groups of people and dupe them into thinking they are being entertained whilst surreptitiously giving them huge dollops of truths on huge risky subjects... race, AIDS, poverty; musicals go there. The stories in this show are true because I don't tell fake stories, that seems pointless because telly does that. Singing is so uplifting, it is literally medicine to me. Singing and dancing. It allows us to be truthful weirdly. But it wouldn't be a Bryony Kimmings show without fucking with form a little, or splicing musical with other things... so hold on to your trousers/sick bowls/chemo drips... this goes ALL over.

Over the past two years I have had the absolute pleasure of meeting some amazing people related to cancer in one way or another; soulful, beautiful, honest people, some still living, some passed now. And when my own son got very ill this year it was those people who helped me most, those who had already travelled into the 'kingdom of the sick' and who could give me directions. Thanks to the amazing cast, crew and writing team... it has been an absolute blast. Enjoy it. It is a true labour of love, sent from us to you as fellow citizens of this confusing, harsh and gorgeous planet earth.

Love BK xx

September 2016

Brian Lobel
Writer

Cancer is both incredibly visible – the subject of major advertising campaigns, extensive reporting on celebrity deaths, a constant source of news and political debate – and deeply under-discussed. Although the days of The Big C (the word that daren't be said) are, thankfully, mostly behind us, cancer still holds a very strange, uncomfortable position in public discussion: we can talk about it, but only using terms and tones of voice which are strictly inspirational or purely mournful, brand-reaffirming and acceptable. Proper. Respectful. *A Pacifist's Guide to the War on Cancer* is our shout (we hope not into the void) that we need, as individuals and a society, to be better at talking about cancer, health, illness, disability, bodies, life and death. Hushed tones help no one, stilted conversation doesn't shrink any tumours.

With *A Pacifist's Guide to the War on Cancer*, we hope to expose and explore (two hours' worth of) the realities of a life lived with cancer – the annoyances, the sounds, the absurdity, the politics – in a way which speaks to both people who have never experienced ill health, and those who have. Perhaps the text will introduce you to new realities, or feel strangely familiar. Maybe your experience with illness (yours or your loved ones) will be (or will have been) vastly different; while we hope to give voice to people not normally heard, the experience of illness is so radically different from person to person, as a company of people with various experiences of cancer, it's our goal to start a conversation, not finish it. There have been amazing works on illness – cancer in particular – but not nearly enough. We hope *A Pacifist's Guide to the War on Cancer* encourages more people to tell their stories honestly and more people to share their opinions publicly.

May we all live in a world in which we let people with cancer be the way they need to be, to be vulnerable when they need to, and strong when they need to, to laugh when they need to, and scream when they need to. And to sing the song that makes them feel welcomed and safe. To sing the song that makes them feel heard.

September 2016

Tom Parkinson
Composer

As well as a million unique individual stories, we wanted, firstly, to present cancer as a social issue that affects all of us. I think the impulse to make a musical about cancer came from music's capacity to create collective experiences. Perhaps music can slot itself into the half-formed and stilted conversations, both public and private, that we are having around cancer, and help to articulate the things that are not readily accessible in words. Music is also good at articulating emotional drama, the highs and lows that characterise illness and the shifting relationships to our bodies. As well as being faithful to the emotional experience of cancer, we wanted to create a musical and sonic universe for the show that had concrete relationships to the disease, which required a compositional continuity between my role and that of Lewis, the sound designer. Harmony is slowly pulled out of a recording of a hospital ventilation system; the pulsing ambience of the waiting room subtly changes key as a scene falls into a song; instead of motivic development in traditional terms, cells of rhythmic and melodic material metastasize throughout the show.

The medical community have been wonderfully accommodating of our research trips and, without exception, have accepted the terms of our project with open and supportive minds. Brian Lobel (writer) and I had a great visit to a hospital in Birmingham, where I conducted a teenage patient, her mum and a nurse in an improvised jam with half a dozen, surprisingly dynamic, chemo machines. Through the many conversations that we have had with patients and their families and with medical professionals, as well as during our own visits to the 'kingdom of the sick', it became clear that cancer has its own sonic universe, from unforgivingly sanitised hospital acoustics to tussles over the jukebox in the common room of the teenage cancer ward to old songs that take on unbearable poignancy. Creating these new songs with Bryony Kimmings has been a massively rewarding process as well as a great responsibility and I hope that they are a fitting tribute to the real stories on which they are based.

September 2016

A PACIFIST'S GUIDE TO THE WAR ON CANCER

A PACIFIST'S GUIDE
TO THE WAR ON CANCER

Book by Bryony Kimmings and Brian Lobel
Music by Tom Parkinson
Lyrics by Bryony Kimmings

OBERON BOOKS
LONDON

WWW.OBERONBOOKS.COM

First published in 2016 by Oberon Books Ltd
521 Caledonian Road, London N7 9RH
Tel: +44 (0) 20 7607 3637 / Fax: +44 (0) 20 7607 3629
e-mail: info@oberonbooks.com
www.oberonbooks.com

PB ISBN: 9781786820600
E ISBN: 9781786820617

Cover image: Bob and Roberta Smith
Back image: Photography Christa Holka
Image Art Direction David Curtis-Ring
Post Production Marcelo Dalle Grave

Characters

EMMA

GIA

LAURA

MARK

STEPHEN

SHANNON

DEREK

STEPHEN'S MUM

DR JONES

LAURA'S HUSBAND

SHANNON'S DAD

DR LACEY

Other nurses, doctors and Blobs played by
members of the company

Voiceovers

BRYONY KIMMINGS

GIA JONES

LARA HAZEL

LARA VIETCH

VICTORIA REILY

BILLY REILY

*This text went to press before the end of rehearsals
and so may differ slightly from the play as performed.*

Part 1

In the black out, a voiceover.

BRYONY: *(Voiceover.)* Hi it's Bryony Kimmings. Welcome to the theatre. A room full of people who have cancer, who have had cancer, who have lost people to cancer and who will get cancer in the future.

I know, heavy right.

Here's a question. Why don't we talk about illness and death more? You personally might, congratulations, but as a society we suck at it, and this has ramifications in how we medicate, treat and talk to people.

How could you make a show about illness and death without risking no one coming? Well, the language surrounding cancer is weird. Fierce battles, Brave Warriors. Inspirational survivors. It all sounds like what you say to sick people if you are really uncomfortable with talking honestly about illness.

So it would be best to make a show about cancer that DIDN'T do any of that. And so it wasn't boring or depressing… we would make it into a nutty weirdo of a musical.

Music begins.

Lights up.

Smokey back light comes on.

Let's follow a single mum's cancer story; broke and a bit dappy and, of course, hasn't seen this coming…

EMMA steps into the backlight.

Part 1. Meet Emma on a Tuesday.

Front light up. EMMA stands with a baby carrier on her front and a letter in her hand. She wears a watch, carries a bag and wears bright red shoes.

EMMA: *(Singing, almost absentmindedly to herself or the baby.)*

In a moment I'll wake up
We'll be playing in the garden
In a moment we'll be fine
And today won't be a hard one

In a moment little bones
Won't be the stuff of little x-rays…

Suddenly she cuts herself off as she looks at her watch. The band falters. It's funny.

EMMA: FUCK! I hate rush hour. We can't be late! Come on. Fingers Crossed!

She hurries off, pissed off with herself. Music begins and people flood the stage on their way to work.

Fingers Crossed

Good morning world
What a mediocre day
I hope that nothing happens 'til
I'm headed back this way

Excuse me miss
Could you move your bag
It's just it's taking up the seat
I've missed three trains to nab

Hello shop-keep
I'll never catch your name
I'll have my usual paper, fags
And can of Coke again

Nice to see you mate
I can't stop to talk

I'm busy faking being busy
Cue determined walk

Everything is fine
I mustn't moan, I mustn't moan
I could be dying of that cancer in a bed alone
Don't think about statistics, never trust TV
I'll just focus on the person's shoes in front of me

As I board this train
I push my panic down
I won't let you see anxiety
Just read and frown

Get out the way
I've got to get to school
Then the vets and the dry cleaners
And the swimming pool

Excuse me please
Could you take my pram?
You are such a strapping lad
And living legend of a man

Please get out the way
This isn't fun
I'm so busy, fucking busy
Cue determined run!

Everything is fine
I mustn't moan, I mustn't moan
I could be dying of that cancer in a bed alone
Don't think about statistics, never trust TV
I'll just focus on the mobile phone in front of me

Fingers crossed, make a wish
What gruesome game of chance is this?
Cross your chest, count one in three
And pray it doesn't grow in me

Why won't he call?
He doesn't like me back
I bet he's swiping right already
On his dating app

I'm super duper stressed
Could it get any worse?
I think I literally just might have
Made a blood vessel burst

Right that's it
Not going in today
I know I'm due to get
The sack this morning anyway

Nice to see you babe
I can't leave this queue
I've got the moany groany
Grumble version of the flu

Everything is fine
I mustn't moan, I mustn't moan
I could be dying of that cancer in a bed alone
Don't think about statistics, never trust TV
I'll just focus on the mobile phone in front of me

Fingers crossed, make a wish
What gruesome game of chance is this?
Cross your chest, count one in three
And pray it doesn't grow in me

ME ME ME ME ME ME ME ME ME ME ME ME ME
ME ME ME ME ME ME ME ME ME ME ME ME ME
ME ME ME

GIA: Excuse me sorry
    Can you repeat that please?
    I don't think I can quite
    Exactly what you mean

LAURA: Is there any news?
I can feel a change
I swear I feel my body
Getting better again

MARK: Goodbye old flat
I'm off to hospital
I'll have to take a cab
The street's impossible

STEPHEN: I'll bring my body here
But keep my soul away

SHANNON: I can't face it
I could do without this today

ENSEMBLE: *(Quietly as they disperse.)* Everything is fine
I mustn't moan, I mustn't moan
I could be dying of that cancer in a bed alone
Don't think about statistics, never trust TV
I'll just focus on the mobile phone in front of me
Fingers crossed

EMMA: *(Speaking to the receptionist.)* Emma Kenworthy.

ENSEMBLE: Make a wish

EMMA: *(Speaking.)* I'm here with baby Owen.

ENSEMBLE: What gruesome game of chance is this?

EMMA: *(Speaking.)* We're here for some tests.

ENSEMBLE: Cross your chest, count one in three

EMMA: *(Speaking.)* We will be out of here by 11 right?

ENSEMBLE: And pray it doesn't grow in me

They sit on their chairs and freeze.

EMMA: Oh okay, I'll just sit and wait here then.

As she sits the waiting room comes to life. The NURSE has a monotone voice.

NURSE: Name?

LAURA: Laura Graham.

NURSE: Date of birth?

LAURA: 3rd October 1975.

NURSE: Oncology department?

LAURA: Ovarian.

NURSE: Thanks Laura. Your doctor asked me to give you this.

The scene freezes.

LAURA: Hospices. Well that's a load of rubbish, so…

Unfreeze.

NURSE: Name? Date of birth?

MARK: Mark Phillips. 30th March '69.

NURSE: Oncology Department?

MARK: *(Inaudibly.)* Lung.

NURSE: Sorry?

MARK: *(Louder.)* Respiratory… *(Annoyed.)* Lung.

The scene freezes. MARK swears. Unfreeze. A phone rings with the 'Sex and the City' theme tune ringtone.

STEPHEN: *(Answering his phone.)* Hi Mum…

The NURSE approaches him.

STEPHEN: Stephen Eric Gowlett. Mum, just give me a couple of minutes.

NURSE: Date of birth?

STEPHEN: 24/9/90.

NURSE: Department?

STEPHEN: Mum…

NURSE: Department?

STEPHEN hangs up.

STEPHEN: Sorry. Urology.

Freeze.

STEPHEN: I can't do everything at once!

Unfreeze.

The NURSE passes EMMA and she tries to get their attention. A cleaner, DEREK, mops around EMMA.

DEREK: You'll be alright, love.

GIA: Gia James, November 4th 1985, soft tissue sarcoma.

NURSE: Cheer up Gia, it might never happen.

Freeze.

GIA: *(Writing in her book.)* Now I'm not saying that cancer is a turn off, but even the cops won't come near me. Radical feminist geek and riddled with it. Are you sure THIS black life matters?!

Unfreeze.

NURSE: Name?

SHANNON: Shannon McGuiness.

Freeze.

SHANNON: I've just turned eighteen and I'm twenty weeks pregnant. Here for some hardcore genetic test results for my baby. Desperately craving celery today. Weird.

Unfreeze.

A DOCTOR comes on to take EMMA's baby away for tests.

DOCTOR: We are going to take baby for his tests now. We will be sedating him and we do ask parents to wait outside, less distressing. It will be a couple of hours.

Freeze.

EMMA: Please don't take my baby. Please don't take him away.

Unfreeze.

TANNOY: *(They stand in turn.)* Can patients James, Phillips, Graham, McGuiness, Gowlett and *(Rustle of paper.)* Kenworthy *(She stumbles up.)* come to the Level 5 waiting room to enter the appointments queuing system.

The patients grid out; exiting the stage making a grid formation across the floor as they leave.

EMMA: *(Mumbling.)* Sorry do you know where... Level 5...?

EMMA tries to go through the door and fails.

EMMA: For god's sake! Where am I meant to be going? They told me to come to the oncology reception. Why would we be in oncology?! I don't think I even know what cancer is!

A BLOB comes on. It speaks with a lisp.

Cancer Cell

BLOB: A cancer cell is an ordinary cell that decides it must mutate
It grows and grows and doesn't switch off, abnormal cell mistake
It doubles and doubles and picks up speed and it makes a little mass
This mass becomes a tumour – sorry if this is crass
The tumour steals a blood supply, danger starts to climb
Chemo, radio, surgery works, well, some of the time
The tricky part comes when the cancer spreads, through blood through lymph through bone
Metastasising rapidly – that's when you know that it's grown

EMMA: What?

BLOB: A cancer cell is an or–

EMMA: No, stop, please. Just tell me where I am.

Another BLOB has entered.

BLOB 2: You're in the Kingdom.

EMMA: What Kingdom?

BLOB 2: The Kingdom of the Sick.

The cast blasts through the upstage doors.

Kingdom of the Sick

Seeping down your leg like a oil slick
Shudder down your spine with an ice-cold stick
Hollowing your stomach to a darkest pit
Crazy like a lunatic

Whack you round the head with a swinging brick
Double up your blood 'til it's mighty thick
Can't quite figure out the politic
Welcome to the Kingdom of the Sick!

Not the kiss of death but a hefty lick
Jumping on your nerves like a pogo stick
Take a pound of flesh with an evil trick
Subtle as an icepick

Whack you round the head with a swinging brick
Double up your blood 'til it's mighty thick
Can't quite figure out the politic
Welcome to the Kingdom of the Sick!

Running full throttle makes your breath go quick
Suicidal bag like a bomb go tick
I'm a firecracker dare to light my wick
Me so toxic

Mother nature mother fucker evil prick
Blinded by the force of a sideways kick
No rhyme no reason no arithmetic
Welcome to the Kingdom of the Sick!

Underneath the characters who are speak-singing in the next section, the ensemble sing:

Shaaa dooo
Shaaa dooo
Shaaa dooo
Shaaa dooo
Shaaa dooo
Shaaa dooo
Shaaa dooooooooo

STEPHEN: The sort of place you find others publicly holding your testicle
A sea of opening and closing curtains that don't cancel sound at all

MARK: So utterly judgmental this place as you wheeze and cough and strain
Drowning in a sea of angry stares and sanctimonious blame

SHANNON: Where family histories are complex and genes a life-long curse
You get to choose your fate between bad and even worse

GIA: Where positive is negative, and negative is great
They speak a different language here and they expect you to translate

Not the kiss of death but a hefty lick
Jumping on your nerves like a pogo stick
Take a pound of flesh with an evil trick
Subtle as an icepick

Whack you round the head with a swinging brick
Double up your blood 'til it's mighty thick

Can't quite figure out the politic
Welcome to the Kingdom of the Sick!

Aaaah
Aaaah
Aaaah
Aaaah
Welcome to the Kingdom of the Sick!

It lands EMMA back into a queue. She shakes her head as it seems normal again. They all take tickets, except for EMMA, and sit down. She sits down too.

STEPHEN: Hi Mum… Yeah, hi Mum, I can't really talk right now *(Hushes his voice.)* I'm at the hospital. Love you, bye.

EMMA: It was just a shadow, it was just a bruise, it was just a piece of fluff on the x-ray machine.

DEREK: Are you alright there? Mrs Kenworthy isn't it?

EMMA: How do you know my name?

DEREK: I pretty much know everyone around here love.

EMMA: Yes I'm fine, I'm just not sure how the system works but I'm trying to keep up with my baby's tests.

DEREK: It can be confusing. But hey, at least the little one will never remember.

TANNOY: Will patients James, Philips, Graham, McGuiness, Gowlett and Kenworthy all make their way to waiting room 3 on Level 6.

EMMA: What?! Where now?

DEREK: Here take a ticket and stick with them, they can show you the ropes.

EMMA: Thank you!

She chases after the patients who grid off. She follows them as best she can but doesn't get through the door – a BLOB stops her. She holds its hand as it makes her watch STEPHEN. STEPHEN's phone rings.

STEPHEN: Hi Mum.

STEPHEN'S MUM: *(As she walks through the door.)* Hi Stephen.

STEPHEN: Mum!!

> *DR JONES enters.*

STEPHEN'S MUM: I've been looking everywhere for you.

DR JONES: Stephen Gowlett? Number 4?

STEPHEN'S MUM: Here!

STEPHEN: Erm here.

DR JONES: Take a seat.

> *They both sit down on his seat and he ends up sitting on his mum's lap, then moves to the next seat.*

DR JONES: I just need to race you through some of these forms.

STEPHEN'S MUM: I could fill in the form if it's quicker?

STEPHEN: Mum I've got this.

DR JONES: Stephen let's speak privately.

STEPHEN'S MUM: Can I ask a quick question?

STEPHEN: Mum! Go on doctor.

DR JONES: Now. Sperm banking…. We recommend you do this before chemo begins today, as it can have a permanent effect on your fertility.

STEPHEN'S MUM: Oh god!

STEPHEN: Mum please!

DR JONES: If you want to do that, the time is now, before we start today.

STEPHEN'S MUM: Yes!

STEPHEN: Mum!

STEPHEN'S MUM: Well you will, won't you Stephen?

STEPHEN: Mum!

STEPHEN'S MUM: Doctor?

STEPHEN: Actually Mum, can you sit in the waiting room? I did ask you not to come today. Mum please.

STEPHEN'S MUM: *(Shrugging off his comment to the doctor.)* He's not himself…

STEPHEN: For fuck's sake Mum! Can we please just get on with the rest of my treatment?

DR JONES: Mrs Gowlett you can grab a cup of tea just down there. Stephen…

STEPHEN and DR JONES exit.

STEPHEN'S MUM: *(Calling after him.)* I bought you some pajamas.

She exits.

EMMA: *(Singing but again to herself as if to reassure.)*
In a moment I'll wake up
They'll say they muddled up the system
In a moment we'll be home
We won't be here in this kingdom

The trudge interrupts EMMA's song. Heavy sounds of footsteps and chains, the exit signs flash – it scares EMMA as it approaches. She comes to the centre and gets whirled up in the circle…

EMMA: *(To the people in the trudge.)* Oh god!
Oh what now! Excuse me can you tell me where you're going. Sorry, what is all this stuff? Is this treatment?! Excuse me…Where are you going?

GIA: Chemo suite.

EMMA: Can I come with you to see?

GIA: Get down! *(Sound of gun shot.)* Okay, brace yourself. Let's go.

The whole world spins and EMMA joins the whirlpool.

My Poor Body

GIA: What's this? (What's what)
　　　What's that?
　　　Hands off! (Off what)
　　　Don't poke me with that
　　　My oh my

　　　One hit! (Man down)
　　　Come back
　　　Blast off! (Blast up)
　　　Don't give me that chat
　　　I could cry

　　　My poor body my poor poor body my poor poor body my
　　　oh my
　　　My poor body my poor poor body my my poor poor body
　　　my oh my

　　　Stand still! (Watch out)
　　　No flack
　　　I'm done! (Damn straight)
　　　Don't follow the pack
　　　My oh my

　　　Bi-beep! (Ding dong)
　　　Click clack
　　　What now? (Sit down)
　　　Man cut me some slack
　　　I could cry

　　　My poor body my poor poor body my my poor poor body
　　　my oh my
　　　My poor body my poor poor body my my poor poor body
　　　my oh my

GIA swaps places with EMMA and for a moment she is being touched by all the doctors.

So you can keep your preaching
And your holy rolling
Because I'm just trying to survive
And I will take these pinpricks
And your curtain twitching
I'm so tired I could cry
Touch me one more time and die

What's this? (What's what)
What's that?
Hands off! (Off what)
Don't poke me with that
My oh my

So you can keep your preaching
And your holy rolling
Because I'm just trying to survive
And I will take these pinpricks
And your curtain twitching
To have control is such a lie

GIA grabs EMMA and shakes her. A BLOB comes on and stands behind her.

Cross my heart don't want to
Cross my heart don't want to
Cross my heart don't want to die...

EMMA breaks free and is startled by the BLOB who keeps her in the room.

TANNOY: Group Therapy. Starting now in room 9. Thank you.

LAURA: Not seeing my daughter very often is the worst.

STEPHEN: Having to keep it a secret from work, that's really hard.

MARK: Not being able to go out and get fucking wankered when I feel like it.

He exits.

LAURA: He's an idiot.

GIA: By far the worst is the positivity police.

LAURA: Nothing wrong with positive mental attitude.

They all look at EMMA.

EMMA: Um I'm just waiting for some results.

SHANNON smiles at her and beckons. The BLOB pushes her forward and then blobs off.

SHANNON: One of the first things you have to get used to is how everyone else treats you. People love to use your tragedy as a springboard for their emotions.

EMMA: How do you mean?

SHANNON: Hmmm okay. These are the friends I like the most... When everyone is just being normal. Just here with me making the best of it.

The patients pretend to be SHANNON's friends, chatting over each other – they are laughing and joking.

SHANNON: Absolutely no one is giving me the cancer face.

SHANNON makes the cancer face, then all the patients do it.

SHANNON: These are the friends that I'm finding more difficult. Overbearing friends with strong ideas on what I should or shouldn't do with my body.

They now have grapes and begin to pass them to SHANNON, popping them into her mouth and saying how good they are for her. She is refusing them but they just keep coming. She spits them all out.

SHANNON: These are the friends I can't be around.

They put the grapes down and pick up the flowers.

SHANNON: The ones with the aggressive sorrow.

They begin to pound the flowers into their hands, like they're holding baseball bats. They look sad.

They begin to sing 'My Friend' and sing this eight times. They begin to pound the flowers faster and faster until they smash them over their own heads. All the flowers go to bits.

SHANNON: I imagine all the things I'd like to do with their flowers.

They all laugh, including EMMA.

EMMA: Oh god I had no idea!

SHANNON: Yeah…

STEPHEN'S MUM enters.

STEPHEN'S MUM: Stephen? I bought you some grapes darling…

STEPHEN: Mum!

They all leave gridding swiftly out.

EMMA: *(Taking a deep breath, again singing to herself, slightly more wobbly about it all this time.)*
In a moment I'll wake up
They'll tell me we aren't meant to be here
In a moment he'll be fine…

TANNOY: Patient Graham to consultant room 7. Patient Graham to consultant room 7. Thank you.

LAURA enters immediately as does her DOCTOR from the opposite door. They stand facing each other across the space. LAURA is beaming.

EMMA: She looks happy. That's the kind of face you want to see. Please show me something good.

DOCTOR: So Laura…

LAURA: So doctor…

DOCTOR: Have you had time to think?

Beat. Music quietly begins, just a bass pulse.

DOCTOR: Laura, as suspected the tumour was unresponsive to the treatment. There are no known further options.

LAURA: It was my daughter's birthday yesterday. She's nine years old.

DOCTOR: Laura I think it's time to look at that hospice information.

LAURA: But there could be something out there. An unknown option.

DOCTOR: Short of a miracle, this IS your only option.

LAURA: The miracle.

DOCTOR: Laura.

LAURA: The miracle cure!

Miracle

DOCTOR: You're not listening to me
Or anything I say
I'm telling you that you have to go to the hospice
But you are miles away

LAURA rips off her dress and reveals a sparkling Seventies jump suit.

LAURA: Shake it down
Hot pursuit
Look around
Find a route

Shake it down
Hot pursuit
Look around
Find a route

The ensemble enter, dressed in Seventies wigs and clothes.

DOCTOR: You are making this impossible
It's hard for you I know

There isn't anything else that we can do for you
It's going to grow and grow

ENSEMBLE and LAURA: Shake it down
Hot pursuit
Look around
Find a route

Shake it down
Hot pursuit
Look around
Find a route

LAURA: Hey Mr Doctor, I'm feeling physical
The only word I heard
That word was Miracle

Hey Mr Doctor
Drugs galore
Do me a favour
Find the cure
Find the cure
F F F find the cure
Find the cure
Find the cure
F F F find the cure

Miracle Miracle Miracle Cure
Miracle Miracle Miracle Cure
Just to check your language and just to be sure
Miracle Miracle Miracle Cure

DOCTOR: You are truly deluded
I can't hold your gaze
You need to look in my eyes as I say this
You're in the last stage

ENSEMBLE and LAURA: Shake it down

Hot pursuit

Look around

Find a route

Shake it down

Hot pursuit

Look around

Find a route

Hey Mr Doctor, I'm feeling physical

The only word I heard

That word was Miracle

Hey Mr Doctor

Drugs galore

Do me a favour

Find the cure

Find the cure

F F F find the cure

Find the cure

Find the cure

F F F find the cure

The ensemble exits.

Miracle Miracle Miracle Cure

Miracle Miracle Miracle Cure

Miracle Miracle Miracle Cure

DOCTOR: There was the faintest glimmer

LAURA: Every shining shimmer

DOCTOR: But it's fading fast

LAURA: Could be a miracle

DOCTOR: The faintest glimmer

LAURA: Every shining shimmer

DOCTOR: But it's fading fast

LAURA: I need a miracle

EMMA: *(Speaking.)* You can do it Laura.

LAURA: What?

EMMA: Anything is possible.

LAURA: I don't know what you're talking about.

LAURA exits. EMMA tries to chase after her but the door is locked again; she bangs it angrily.

MARK enters to floating guitar strings and heavy breathing. The colour of the space changes, smoke wafts on. He is a lonely cowboy. He snakes the stage. As he does so the BLOBS follow him on, snaking behind him slowly. EMMA watches.

Lonesome

MARK: Ain't nobody ever felt lonesome like I do
Ain't nobody ever felt lonesome

Ain't nobody ever felt vulnerable like I do
Ain't nobody ever felt lonesome

And I can't understand
No I can't understand

I've tried I've tried
You pushed me aside
I can't wait for you no more

Ain't nobody ever felt confused like I do
Ain't nobody ever felt lonesome

Ain't nobody ever felt loveless like I do
Ain't nobody ever felt lonesome

And I can't understand
No I can't understand

I've tried I've tried
You pushed me aside
I can't wait for you no more

I've tried I've tried
You pushed me aside
I can't wait for you no more

He comes to rest and the BLOBS assemble around him.

EMMA: Who are you waiting for?

MARK: My daughter.

MARK pulls out a fag and starts to smoke it. EMMA rolls her eyes, she is angry. The music stays floating underneath.

EMMA: Do you think it's a good idea for you to be smoking?

MARK: What?!

EMMA: I mean, it looks like you've done yourself enough damage. Some people *(Gesturing after LAURA.)* have absolutely no control over their cancer and there you are making yours worse. You should be ashamed.

MARK: I beg your fucking pardon.

EMMA: You heard me.

MARK: I'm only going to say this once, and I don't mean to be rude, because unlike you I don't shout at strangers, so prick up your ears and pay attention. Yeah I've smoked for over thirty years. Yeah I've put myself in the path of every carcinogen out there: asbestos from building sites, tar, environmental toxins of the fucking north, a terrible diet and all manner of other damage that poverty brings. Yeah I know you look at me and see a jobless waster, a self inflicted drain on the NHS, a terrible absent father whose daughter no longer gives a fuck… all painfully true. BUT… if you think that by being ill, I am somehow taking chemo out of your sick baby's veins, then you don't understand the NHS and the socialist principles that created it. I've

paid my fucking taxes, lady, so fuck off and let me smoke
my cigarette in peace.

*The BLOBS spin out to a semi-circle around him. MARK continues
to smoke his cigarette and makes his way off. EMMA is shaken and
upset. She walks past a BLOB to try another door. It follows her;
she stops and turns back and it hides. Again she walks, this time
three BLOBS follow. Again she looks, and they hide. As she looks at
them the other three surround her. They spin around and chatter at
her and push and scare her. She escapes the BLOBS and lands in the
kitchen, holding SHANNON's bump.*

SHANNON: Twenty weeks.

EMMA: What?

SHANNON: Twenty weeks.

EMMA is dazed.

SHANNON: I saw you in the waiting room, didn't I? Little boy.
Is he ill?

Beat.

EMMA: I'm not sure.

SHANNON: Do they think he might have cancer?

EMMA: Well, um… um. Are you in treatment? While pregnant?
Sorry that's a really personal question.

SHANNON: No it's okay, I'm very used to it. I have had cancer
in the past. My Mum also recently died of cancer. We both
share a very rare genetic disorder. Today I find out if my
baby has it.

EMMA: Gosh.

SHANNON: Yeah…

SHANNON: Are you with me? What is it?

EMMA: Yes. They do. They think my boy may have cancer.

EMMA lurches forward. She holds her hands to her mouth in disbelief. A sound rings out and she begins to sway.

SHANNON: I'm so sorry.

EMMA stumbles backwards; she is being dragged out of the scene by an unknown force. The people she has met that morning trudge towards her through the doors.

SHANNON: Are you alright?

Part 2

There is no interval, Part 2 begins immediately. There is a loud whooshing noise and EMMA is flung around straight into the path of the oncoming people. Like a hyper-flashback. She hits into them and they bash past her, under their breath they are saying 'Welcome to the Kingdom of the Sick'. At the end of the line up there is a BLOB. EMMA has been watching the queue exit the stage but the BLOB bashes her again and she spins round right into her son in a hospital cot, with two DOCTORS flagging the gurney. The lights suddenly change to sterile eerie colours.

DOCTOR: *(The DOCTOR's voice is long and weird.)* I'm afraid we found some abnormalities in Owen's blood. We need to take him for a biopsy. Prepare to stay the night.

The gurney spins so EMMA is now upstage.

EMMA: This can't be happening... *(Starting to speak sing.)* In a moment...

The gurney slips out of her hands and her voice stops the space and its sound goes long and slow as she staggers forward confused.

BRYONY: *(Voiceover.)* After the denial of possible cancer wears thin, a torrent of emotions unleash. The kick of adrenaline. Swiftly followed by a deep and uncontrollable rage.

Part 2 Emma. The darkest hours of Wednesday morning. Or what I like to call 'the bubbling supernatural force of motherhood unleashed'.

EMMA suddenly channels a supernatural force and she makes all the doors in the space swing with it. She is all-powerful. A blob inflates at the side of the space and she watches it as it makes a screeching noise. Then she flings all the doors open as if to show the blob her powers, and they stay open for the rest of Part 2. We see the stage crew, they are dressed as porters. The ensemble come spiralling out and gather around her. Each does tiny little methodical jobs with their hands, organising in an abstract way. EMMA stands in the centre thinking, plotting. She quietens the people as she listens to what each of them are doing; she is making quick decisions, moving her arms to stop and start them. Suddenly they stop and they sing. She has lost control of them, she doesn't want to hear it, she puts her hands over her ears.

Fingers Crossed Dark Reprise

ENSEMBLE: Fingers crossed, make a wish
What gruesome game of chance is this?

EMMA then switches them back on, they move more frantically. Another blob begins to inflate. She gets annoyed with them and sends them all swirling in a huge spiral. Toilets come on, and a sink. STEPHEN has stopped and is rubbing his head. EMMA makes the swirl stop and all the ensemble hit an imaginary wall, apart from STEPHEN and his MUM who are arguing. EMMA is in a trance. STEPHEN and his MUM's voices echo as if they are in a huge space with no ceiling. Weird. Underneath them is a strange digital beeping monotony.

STEPHEN: Mum, I'm not having this conversation with you again.

STEPHEN'S MUM: I'm just saying, Stephen, it's probably stress that brought this on in the bloody first place.

STEPHEN: Mum I have to work, okay. I mean who's going to pay my rent? You?

STEPHEN'S MUM: Just come back home, we've got everything you need.

STEPHEN: What I need is to not have cancer.

STEPHEN'S MUM: Darling. I'm afraid that's not possible.

EMMA and STEPHEN: I need to go to the toilet.

Beat. Music begins.

STEPHEN: I asked. No you know what, I told you not to come. But you came anyway, because it's not really about what I want or need, but what makes you happy…

EMMA: *(Singing.)* This can't be happening, it just can't.

STEPHEN: Mum.

EMMA and STEPHEN: It's fine.

STEPHEN: I'm fine. And you don't need to worry about…

STEPHEN catches sight of the fact his hair is falling out. He is shocked.

Castaway

STEPHEN: Standing in a boat on a lake
Looking at reflectivity
I think that you made a mistake
You do not know what's best for me

And I can't see your face
'Cause the boat it is full of debris
But I'm not the boy that you made
I left him on the shore all empty

When I'm no longer a man
And I just feel like a machine
And here pumps my heart in a case
And the boat floats so gently

And it's about time that you knew
That I'm away from you purposefully
So I can be here by myself
Floating through reflectivity

And it's high time I told you that you can stay back from
now on
And it's my time I owe you but you can back track now
I'm gone

Gone mother gone mother gone mother gone mother gone
Gone mother gone mother gone mother gone mother gone

Castaway

STEPHEN'S MUM: *(Calling through the doors.)* Stephen my boy?
Are you alright in there my darling?

STEPHEN: *(Speaking.)* Yeah, I'll be out in a minute.

Under the waves there is calm
Thrashing out will get us nowhere
Sure as the lines on my palm
Sinking to the bottom this pair

And I can't hold you too tight
'Cause you might feel my bones
Boat moving slow through the night
My pockets are full of these stones

And I can't hold my breath
'Cause I'm falling apart at the seams
And I try not think about death
But we both know what this means

And it's about time that you knew
That I'm away from you purposefully
So I can be here by myself
Floating through reflectivity

And it's high time I told you that you can stay back from
now on
And it's my time I owe you but you can back track now
I'm gone

Gone mother gone mother gone mother gone mother gone
Gone mother gone mother gone mother gone mother gone

Castaway

*STEPHEN looks at his hair and cannot cope. He comes out of the
toilet in a panic.*

STEPHEN: Mum. Mum. Mum.

EMMA comes out of the toilet also panicking, shouting.

EMMA: Owen. Owen. Owen. Owen. Owen.

She can't breathe. DEREK enters and tries to calm her down.

DEREK: Come on, Mrs Kenworthy, let's take a second, calm down, calm down.

They all begin to say something under their breath.

EMMA, STEPHEN, STEPHEN'S MUM and DEREK: Me me me me me *(repeated).*

The cast now fly onstage in a fast moving line, each pounding their chests and saying 'Me me me' like they did in the opening number, but much more desperate. The toilets are hurtled off with them. All the cast hit the back wall and almost squash into it and then bash – they fly back into the space into a slim corridor from left to right and they are raving hard. The music is going mental; everyone is trying to be out of their heads. One ACTOR plays all the male parts in this next rave section. The sound lowers and the ravers float. LAURA and the ACTOR are back to back and floating in the air abstracting their voices amongst the ravers.

HUSBAND: We can't do this anymore, Laura. *(Beat.)* Laura, listen to me.

LAURA: I don't know what you mean.

HUSBAND: This. THIS! I can't manage. We can't.

LAURA: Come on.

HUSBAND: Listen!

LAURA: I'm trying.

HUSBAND: We can't sleep at night, we're all so tired. I can't nurse you all night, work all day, drive to trials, hold everything together. We can't keep up with it anymore.

LAURA: So, what! Do you want me to give up? To give in? *(Beat.)* If I go to that hospice, I'll die!

HUSBAND: Silly girl, look around you, this is happening.

The noise comes back in loud as fuck. Another blob starts to inflate. They rave again amongst the crowd. Again the sound lowers and this time the ravers get stuck. SHANNON and the ACTOR this time, casting him in the role of her DAD.

SHANNON: Dad, I have the results.

DAD: Where?

SHANNON: They're in my hand right now.

DAD: I don't know why you need to do this, I really don't.

SHANNON: How can I not know?

DAD: Shannon, your mother never knew. Some things you're not meant to know.

SHANNON: I wish she were here.

DAD: I just don't understand it. How, HOW could you have been so irresponsible?

SHANNON: It's done now, so…

DAD: And if the baby has it? What then? Who do you think's gonna clear up your mess?

SHANNON: I just have to know, one way or the other.

DAD: Well, you've made your bed.

Bash – the rave comes back in, louder than ever. They rave hard, out of their heads. And bash one more time. It lowers, the ravers stop. EMMA flies off the handle at DEREK – she is fucking angry.

EMMA: Sorry what the fuck. Who are you? What the fuck has it got to do with you. He's my son. It's none of your fucking business, and it won't just miraculously be alright… You're just the fucking cleaner, you don't know me… fuck off.

They rave one more time, but slowly now before it peters out. And without music, they are just useless and out of breath and gasping. They can't breathe. They exit slowly trying to catch their breath. EMMA notices MARK as he passes her, even worse than ever. He tries to sing 'Lonesome' to her, a few bars, but it's tragic and impossible to make out. The ensemble all gather in the wings and smoke cigarettes. As they head off a NURSE enters with the baby in their arms wrapped in a blanket. Again their speech is long and monotone.

NURSE: Biopsy's gone up to the lab. It'll be a few hours. Try not to worry. Here are a few pamphlets. He is still sedated; should sleep through the night.

The NURSE hands her the baby and exits. A slow trudge begins backstage, you can hear the heavy footsteps slowly shuffling and see bodies moving behind the open doors. EMMA begins to trudge heavily forwards – she is trying to sing, a sort of fucked up digital version of her reprise plays and she is trying to get words out.

EMMA: *(Singing.)* Moment...
Wake up...
Home...

A line of people trudge in, each cannot talk in some way, shape or form; their mouths are full, they can't shut them, they simply have no energy. The music gets darker, they trudge slowly. Another blob starts to inflate. GIA enters, writing furiously in her diary. By this point EMMA is mirroring her position, staring at her baby, while the trudgers peel off and head out.

SHANNON is the last person to trudge off. She is just about getting words out; the first few words of her song over and over again, until she finds it in her to begin.

SHANNON: *(Singing.)* Mine is such a complicated story

EMMA: Please Mother Nature. Please god.

SHANNON: *(Singing.)* It would make a stranger take a breath

GIA: Please universe. Send me some strength.

SHANNON: *(Singing.)* So I just don't tell anybody

EMMA and GIA: I can't do this anymore.

SHANNON: *(Singing.)* No one wants to be that close to death.
(Speak singing.) Mum...would you have wanted to know?
All those years ago

Peace of Mind

SHANNON: Of all the things I'd leave behind
I didn't have you in my sights
Even being pregnant is so hard to compartmentalise
I just need some peace of mind

Parents, are complicated creatures
They don't sit well with tragic news
It will hurt my father if he knew this
It's Mum not him I need to talk to

Would you have let me go
All those years ago?

Of all the things I'd leave behind
I didn't have you in my sights
Mum I need you though we've said our last goodbyes
I just need some peace of mind

I don't know how long I last here
But isn't that life all the time
If I give my tiny baby
An unknown future just like mine

I can't let you go
No matter what this shows

GIA and EMMA both come forward either side of SHANNON.

Of all the things I'd leave behind
I didn't have you in my sights
Do you think not knowing is anyway to live a life
I will find my peace

EMMA: Can I find my peace

GIA: Will I find my peace

SHANNON: I must find my peace

ALL: I will find my peace of mind

The music morphs and GIA and SHANNON suck backwards in a weird broken walk. EMMA stays front.

EMMA: The hospital at night is a very different place. More bleak. More depressing. Every face you see is thick with sorrow or tiredness. My rage is dulled by the hum of the low level lights. It feels like the walls could suck us in whole. Owen. How long have we been here? Five minutes, five hours, five days? Yesterday time meant nothing. Today it stretches endlessly. Wandering the halls looking for signs.

She shakes out the blanket and the baby isn't in it. She is confused.

EMMA: Owen? Owen? Eat. Sleep. Cry.

She makes her way backwards to the canteen assembling behind her. The whole ensemble are engrossed in iPads. Monotonous music begins.

GIA: *(Scrolling and sighing.)* Arghhhhh stuck in a Facebook spiral… Hotdog legs. Selfie. Marvel characters redrawn to be feminists. Positive affirmation in a flower image. Can't. Get. Out!

SHANNON: Li–Fraumeni Syndrome is a hereditary cancer disorder discovered whilst reviewing 648 rhabdomyosarcoma patients.

LAURA: Miracle cancer cure. *(Deletes and retypes.)* Ovarian cancer miracle. *(Deletes and retypes.)*

STEPHEN: I am sorry for my absence again today from the office, I hope this has not caused any major inconvenience.

MARK: Dear Michaela, it's your dad… I'm sorry it's taken me so long to get back in touch. I've been thinking about you a lot.

GIA: Selfie, selfie. No make-up selfie. Bucket of ice over your head, sign this, bake that, race there, be a survivor… fuck this.

All of their faces are lit.

ENSEMBLE: *(Singing.)* Fuck this
This wasn't what I needed
Fuck this
This wasn't what I wanted
Fuck this
This wasn't what I needed

MARK: I find myself hoping you might miraculously appear on the ward.

SHANNON: Patients are particularly susceptible to rare childhood cancers. Oh god.

STEPHEN: I will be back in tomorrow… Friday… I'll be back next week.

LAURA: Miracle cures ovarian cancer.

EMMA: Look at them all. Eye deep in regrets and prayers and desperation. Nowhere to go but the canteen. The digital world is a cruel place. I daren't look. I mustn't look.

She picks up her own iPad and then slams it down again.

GIA: 'Picturing Life Beyond Cancer', a positive user-generated photo essay collecting positive stories and images from positive cancer survivors. Urgh! Fuck this.

ENSEMBLE: *(Singing.)* Fuck this
This wasn't what I wanted
Fuck this
This wasn't what I needed

STEPHEN: I hurt my wrist saving a child from a burning building… no.

MARK: Michaela, I'm not sure if you've seen my message, not sure if I'm in spam or whatever, I'm not even sure how this fucking thing works.

LAURA: Left-field shamanic miracle cancer treatment. *(Deletes and retypes.)* Last ditch chanting cancer cure.

EMMA: Cancer is a fucking cunt. What kind of god gives children cancer… This is horrific. Nothing can prepare you for this. *(She puts the iPad down again.)* Fuck this.

ALL: *(Singing.)* Fuck this
Don't tell me this is living
Fuck this
All taking and no giving
Fuck this
I'm sick of all the silence
Fuck this
It's enough to make us violent

SHANNON: Childhood cancer survival rates.

MARK: Darling I just wanted to tell you that I love you. And I'm so fucking sorry.

STEPHEN: What am I doing? In all honesty I have recently been diagnosed with cancer.

LAURA: *(Noticing everyone whispering about miracles behind her.)* Okay. *(She takes a deep breath.)* Hospices in South London.

EMMA: This isn't going away. You have to look Emma. Look at what you are up against. *(She starts to Google.)*

GIA: That's it! Why does it always have to be positive? Do you know what…This is a photo of my cancerous body.

My poor poor, body…
My skinny fat, body
My kinky hair don't care body

My over-35 and single, while everyone else is co-habitating and breeding body
My high-functioning with a chronic illness travels to my clinical trial once a month body
My understands cancer is but one of the things that makes me weird, I'm intersectional as shit, body

EMMA: *(Typing.)* Bone cancer in babies.

GIA: I am writing this comment on your positive photo competition for Audre Lorde and her breasts, for Lucy Grealey and her face. For Susan and her bone marrow, Stephen Sutton MBE and his colon, and Viv and her cervix, and…

SHANNON: Jade Goody and her cervix.

GIA: And Henrietta and her cervix, and…

STEPHEN: Donna Summer and her lung.

LAURA: Bowie and his liver.

GIA: Yeah… and even Lance with his fucking ball. And Freddie and his AIDS, and Robin and his depression, and Whitney and her drugs, and…

MARK: Amy and her drink.

EMMA: *(Not involved, engrossed in Googling.)* Oh god. Oh fuck.

GIA: YEAH! And all the un-famous, normal-ass people who are sitting at home, and feeling guilty about NOT feeling positive… Do. Not. Tell. People. How. To. Deal with their cancer. Period.

STEPHEN: Send it.

Vulnerability Club

Give me mistakes
Give me heartbreaks
All of this fake
Not the man made

Give me brutal
Give me crucial
The unusual
Just be truthful

Pain makes me ecstatic
I revel in the dramatic

'Glitter makes me fantastic'
It's not the mother fucking Life Aquatic

Give me real fears
Give me wet tears
Give me bloodbath
Give me aftermath

Give me sympathy
Give me empathy
Surely honesty's
The best policy

It's not cool to think that
You are something gross to look at
Bald head, one ball, back fat
Carpe diem that you ass-hat

Like like like LOL True Love
I like you just the way you are… well kind of

Like like like LOL True Love
Deep Dark and Real – vulnerability club

EMMA: *(Still static and Googling, singing to her iPad, needing help.)*
Give me the truth
Give me the proof
Don't give me excuse
Or rose-tinted hues

This is desperate
This is reckless
Do not mess with
Something so precious

Watch the hours just flying by
Tomorrow is a different type of sky

Terrified I cannot lie

EMMA grabs GIA and SHANNON for support.

Hold me close I think I'll fucking cry

They let her cling to them for the rest of the song. They understand.

ALL: Like like like LOL True Love
I like you just the way you are… well kind of

Like like like LOL True Love
Deep Dark and Real – vulnerability club

Give me back my baby
Give me back control
Give me back my body
Give me back my soul

Give me back my ignorance
Give me back my bliss
Give me back reality
I don't like this

Give me back my testicle
Give me back my hair
Give me back my energy
Give me back my air

Give me back my sanity
Give me back my wife
Give me back my body
Give me back my life

As a group they chant together. This should be sad, and quite spooky. Like the toughness is coming back to them, like they are wading through thickness.

VUL
NER
ABI
LITY

VUL
NER

ABI

LITY

They fight against it and try to dance again. EMMA is okay, not joining in but trying to be positive.

Pain makes me ecstatic

I revel in the dramatic

'Glitter makes me fantastic'

It's not the mother fucking Life Aquatic

Like like like LOL True Love

I like just the way you are… well kind of

Like like like LOL True Love

Deep Dark and Real – vulnerability…

TANNOY: Paging Emma Kenworthy. Paging Emma Kenworthy. We need to take your son for an urgent MRI scan, please return to the ward immediately.

Smash straight into the MRI.

Part 3

Again there is no interval. Part 3 begins immediately with an MRI for three solid minutes.

Out of the MRI comes a refrain sung by STEPHEN and his MUM, LAURA, GIA, SHANNON and MARK.

CAST: I'm sorry I was never good enough for you.
Good enough for you.

Then back to the MRI for another thirty seconds as the foley table comes in. Then it snaps off to silence. Straightaway this plays.

DOCTOR: *(Voiceover.)* Alright Mrs Kenworthy, we'll get that up to radiology and results to you as soon as possible. Gather up your things, we will take baby to the ward and ask you to wait, okay?

EMMA nods. She gets up and walks in a grid around the stage, trying to figure out where to go. You hear the sound of her footsteps through the foley. When she comes to the waiting room she sits next to LAURA. As soon as she sits she is called again so she barely hits the chair.

TANNOY: Mrs Kenworthy to consultant room 7, thank you.

EMMA gets up. She walks to the consultant's room, again in a grid. The diagnosis scene plays out in foley. Unheard, except a few individual words, as underlined.

DR LACEY: Come in, come in. Did you manage to eat?

EMMA: Yes.

DR LACEY: So, the MRI shows us that there is, indeed, a mass on the humerus, that we believe is problematic. Osteosarcoma, a treatable cancer of the bone.

EMMA: Osteo…

DR LACEY: Osteosarcoma. It's okay Emma I have all of this information here for you. The good news is that

46

we don't believe it's spread beyond the humerus which means this mass is treatable. The treatment does involve chemotherapy fortnightly over six months, but you'll have a few <u>options</u> of how to proceed. It's not an easy treatment course, but it is something we administer often.

EMMA cries.

DR LACEY: It's okay, when you're ready. <u>Statistically</u> this has a very high success rate… I would like to start treatment as soon as possible – and we can get you in as early as Wednesday to start the first round.

EMMA: Wednesday?

DR LACEY: Wednesday. I know that this is overwhelming, and there are logistics to organise, but you're doing great. Do you have any questions? Not now? It's okay, but let's get Owen checked in for a final few blood tests today, okay?

EMMA: Fine.

DR LACEY: Can I just have you sign this consent and then the nurse and I will take you down?

At the end of the scene EMMA's head crashes down with a huge foley thump, and the DOCTOR removes the chair as she falls off it.

She drags herself screaming to the waiting room, following the same path she came on. As she manages to get onto her chair there is a long pause. LAURA gives her a tissue.

Halfway through her drag DEREK comes behind her and mops where she has dragged herself. He stops by her side.

DEREK: Are you alright Mrs Kenworthy?

She manages a nod.

A blob slowly blows up and it moves some of the patients onto each other's laps in the waiting room.

All of a sudden SHANNON comes bursting through the door holding her test results. She is in disbelief. So very very happy. She dances around the stage, she is exclaiming. She can't believe it. She taps and she taps out of control. As she does the DOCTOR and NURSE wheel in the baby on its gurney. It is attached to a little chemo machine.

SHANNON: Yes! Yes!

EMMA stands up and lunges for SHANNON, grabbing her to make her still.

EMMA: Shut the fuck up!

EMMA passes SHANNON who tries to touch her, but she just flinches. SHANNON feels like a total idiot and starts to walk away, as she does so she tries to silence her tap shoes.

EMMA sits with her head on the side of the baby's cot. She places her hand on the chemo machine and the machine plays the sound of her song 'In a moment'. When she takes her hand off it stops. She does this twice.

She begins a ritual of sorts, starting slowly, placing the contents of her handbag on the floor around the cot, then flowers and the baby's bottle, whilst muttering to herself. She steals flowers from STEPHEN's MUM's bag. Next she throws baby milk powder over the space. Then she cuts her hand open violently to drip blood all over the floor. She is making a spell. As she does so the hospital staff and patients gather around her in a semi-circle, watching, worried. DEREK tries to approach but she screams at him to stay back. Two other large blobs inflate, pushing the crowd closer into her.

EMMA: *(Saying what she wants in the ritual.)* Please Mother Nature, please god. Please universe. Please help my little boy. Give him strength, give him healing, make it not hurt him. Not him. Do not take him to the land of the dead *(Repeating over and over)*.

Stay away from me *(To the ACTORS surrounding her in a semi-circle)*. Take me. Take me. Take me. Take me.

She falters, she cries and drops to her knees. DEREK slowly approaches. Another person brings her a chair. They comfort her. People clear the space (not the blobs) and try to help. The music dies out.

BRYONY: *(Voiceover.)* Pause. Here is where I would like to leave Emma and Owen's story. Thank you. This is where their first day ends. Just as Derek the cleaner is thinking about how to scrub that blood off the floor. Just as the car park gets full all over again. Just as the doctors begin their laborious morning handover. One day. Just a slice. Of real life. Part 3. Getting real.

The verbatim scene plays. Slowly throughout it EMMA listens. She is being surrounded by real people with cancer. As each voiceover plays, the corresponding ACTOR mouths along.

GIA: *(Voiceover.)* Uuh my name is Gia Jones. And I live in Michigan – I'm originally from Michigan.

LARA H [LAURA]: *(Voiceover.)* And during the holiday my tummy started to bloat, really bloat, and I came back and basically what's happened is, and this is the changing thing…

LARA V [SHANNON]: *(Voiceover.)* So I first had cancer when I was one, and um, it was a rhabdomyosarcoma.

VICTORIA [STEPHEN'S MUM]: *(Voiceover.)* Is this a good thing that you should be doing this? This is taking you back to your treatment. Not meant to make a bloody National Theatre play about it, so then they'll give you a programme just to remind you of what you went through, and you've to sit there for two hours and watch it. I mean, I don't think it's very diplomatic, do you? And you've got to pay a ticket to go and watch it.

MARK: *(Voiceover.)* [BREATHING]

LARA H [LAURA]: *(Voiceover.)* I got, I got fluid in my tummy, and that's from the cancer accelerating.

GIA: *(Voiceover.)* I work as an alternative educator, and I have soft tissue sarcoma cancer. Which…

LARA V [SHANNON]: *(Voiceover.)* Part of my story includes the fact that not long after that my mum got ill with cancer and died when she was 27.

MARK: *(Voiceover.)* [BREATHING]

LARA V [SHANNON]: *(Voiceover.)* I just… Whatever happens will happen and I will accept whatever comes. I'm not scared of it – I'm an atheist I don't believe that, I don't believe in heaven or hell.

LARA H [LAURA]: *(Voiceover.)* And, I was, I think given three to five years, but I…it hasn't really been mentioned since and I don't really…I've been in denial for three years because that's been my way of dealing with it, well that's a load of rubbish, so.

More audio mixing sounds. The characters grasp for words in the air.

ACTOR PLAYING SHANNON: That's how far Shannon is, in the show.

LARA V [SHANNON]: *(Voiceover.)* Is it? Okay, yeah that – I mean that's… I've never been twenty weeks pregnant so I don't know, but I can imagine that I would find it too difficult to abort by that point.

ACTOR PLAYING SHANNON: You'd have a good little bump by then as well.

VICTORIA [STEPHEN'S MUM]: *(Voiceover.)* So that's like, you being a prisoner of war, in a, in a, camp, and then somebody's filmed it, and they play it back to you, and you have to pay to go and watch it, to make you suffer. Don't you think? Who's the lady that's asked you to do this?

BILLY [STEPHEN]: *(Voiceover.)* Oh, Bryony.

VICTORIA [STEPHEN'S MUM]: *(Voiceover.)* Oh, Bryony. Has Bryony got any brains? She probably hasn't!

GIA: *(Voiceover.)* About what?

ACTOR PLAYING GIA: How I'm saying it? The line?

GIA: *(Voiceover.)* Oh yeah, that's a little too Southern.

ACTOR PLAYING GIA: Too Southern?

GIA: *(Voiceover.)* Yeah.

ACTOR PLAYING GIA: Okay. So how would it be?

GIA: *(Voiceover.)* Hmmm. Can you say it again? Because I'm trying to figure out what it is that makes it sound Southern.

ACTOR PLAYING GIA: Southern. Okay. Now I'm not saying that cancer is off putting to potential sexual partners, but even the cops won't come near me.

GIA: *(Voiceover.)* That one was better.

ACTOR PLAYING GIA: That one was better.

EMMA: What happens to all of them?

BRYONY: *(Voiceover.)* It is very hard to finish their stories as they continue on, as lives do. But… Gia still lives with her cancer. She has found a full-time teaching gig and she hopes that the clinical trial that she's on will never end, and that the experimental drug she takes will keep being produced.

ACTOR playing GIA takes off the costume and exits.

Shannon is currently receiving proton beam therapy in Florida for her sixth cancer. She hopes this will be her last cancer for quite some time.

ACTOR playing SHANNON takes off the costume and exits.

Stephen is better, cancer free. He works, and is happy, most of the time. He and his mother both individually hope they never have to have a conversation about sperm banking again.

ACTORS playing STEPHEN and his MUM take off their costumes and exit.

Mark I don't know. Because I never heard from him again. I hope he managed to speak to his daughter but I suspect that he didn't.

ACTOR playing MARK takes off his costume and exits.

After three years living with a terminal ovarian cancer diagnosis Laura died, in a hospice, with her family. Laura was an actor and a singer. She told me that she couldn't sing for three years after her diagnosis but in the few months before her death she found her voice again. I wrote this song for her. She approved.

Silly Girl

LAURA: Once upon a lifetime I knew the name
Of every single flower on my Grandma's grave
I would walk around the churchyard
Find a resting place
By my Nana's graveside I was mighty brave

Once upon a growing up I found a voice
Singing out and proud I gave no other voice a choice
I would lay myself upon the line
Found my aggressive phase
In the face of danger I was mighty brave

How times change
How I've changed
Once upon a later life I found a place
Where I could be a mother in a loving space
I'd feel so very fearless and so full of grace
In my daughter's presence I was mighty brave

How times change
How I've changed

Something is different now
A burning desire to flee
Somehow I'm different but how

Extinguished the fire in me

Once upon a nightmare, lay awake at night
Trapped beneath the sheets I find I cannot fight
Pace around the corridors
An empty place
I can't I find the girl who once was mighty brave

How times change
How I've changed

ACTOR playing LAURA takes off her costume and bellypad and hands them to EMMA.

Silly girl
Silly girl
Silly girl silly girl silly girl
Silly girl
Just a girl
Silly girl silly girl silly girl

She exits the stage and sits in the audience.

EMMA: If they are all based on people Bryony, then who am I based on?

BRYONY: *(Voiceover.)* Your character is based on me.

EMMA: *(Slightly annoyed.)* And why am I you? Why don't you just come here and do it yourself?

BRYONY: *(Voiceover.)* I have to be at home. My baby son got very very ill as I wrote this musical. We spent months in hospital. Deep within the Kingdom of the Sick. When he was ill I kept coming back to one thought, why wasn't I ready... why wasn't I ready?

Beat.

ACTOR PLAYING EMMA: I felt like that when my dad passed away. *(The ACTOR may say some personal words about their relative or loved one, if they would like to.)*

Is your son alright now?

BRYONY: *(Voiceover.)* He is much better, thank you.

ACTOR PLAYING EMMA: And what is your son's name?

BRYONY: *(Voiceover.)* Frank. And what was your dad's name?

ACTOR PLAYING EMMA: His name was Steve.

BRYONY: *(Voiceover.)* Frank and Steve.

> There must be so many names in this room. At this point I would like the cast to come back onstage and say the names of anyone they have found in the Kingdom of the Sick or that have passed away, if they would like to remember them.

ACTOR PLAYING EMMA: Okay I can ask… Company would you like to come back?

The ACTORS come back onstage and say the names of people.

BRYONY: *(Voiceover.)* And perhaps people in the audience would say the names of people they would like to mention at this point?

The ACTOR PLAYING EMMA holds the space as members of the audience say the names of people they want to mention.

ACTOR PLAYING EMMA: Thank you. And where would you like to go next?

BRYONY: *(Voiceover.)* This is going to sound weird but can we make the stage a kind of choral garden?

ACTOR PLAYING EMMA: Okay, band?

Pianist begins to play.

ACTOR PLAYING EMMA: Maybe someone could start?

One of the company begins to sing the requiem. The blobs inflate more and move forward, bringing the cast closer to the audience. Some come off the front of the stage. It sustains itself for a while.

BRYONY: *(Voiceover.)* When my baby was really very poorly, all drugged up on steroids and angry as hell, I used to walk him around the village we lived in to keep him asleep. Late at night I would go to the churchyard and cry and beg the universe to save him.

Those that understood me most were the cancer patients I had worked with on this musical. They helped me keep my hope alive when everything else in my life broke. I wanted one such person up on this stage with us each night to do that for us.

A CANCER PATIENT comes onstage, introduces themself and talks about their diagnosis. They read out their hopes. As an example, at the first performance, Sharon Kliszcz read the following:

PATIENT: Hello, my name is Sharon, and I was first diagnosed in 2013. And these are my hopes.

I hope my body can begin to fight back. That my immune system can have the break it needs to repair itself.

I hope my daughter never has to go through this and that it isn't a genetic thing.

I hope we stop bleeding the NHS and I hope the NHS stops bleeding.

I hope one day they will switch everything off for a week in the western world and start again.

I hope to have a cow in my urban back garden without complaints from the neighbours.

I hope to one day understand better why we are here.

ACTOR PLAYING EMMA: Thank you. And then…

BRYONY: *(Voiceover.)* Then our cancer patient would move centre stage and begin our final simple song. Wobbly and a bit scared. But here in a room with complete strangers rooting for them.

PATIENT: Fingers crossed, make a wish
For myself, or those I miss

Fingers crossed, make a wish
For myself, or those I miss

Beat.

BRYONY: *(Voiceover.)* The band would join in… *(The band plays the intro.)* … and then the cast would join in and they would spread around the space intertwining with the crowd who may also want to join.

Four more rounds with music, cast and audience.

ALL: Fingers crossed, make a wish
For myself, or those I miss

Fingers crossed, make a wish
For myself, or those I miss

Fingers crossed, make a wish
For myself, or those I miss

Fingers crossed, make a wish
For myself, or those I miss

BRYONY: *(Voiceover.)* Here we are. Old patients, new patients and future patients in a room. How do we talk about illness and death more?

The cast finish it.

All: Cross your chest, count one in three
In solidarity.

Black out.

9 781786 820600